Avoiding Bear Traps

Easy Macro Factors for Smart Traders

First Edition

I0485045

Kara M. Boniecka

LakeshoreATS, Chicago, IL

Table of Contents

For my amazing mother, who after decades as an elementary school math teacher has taken on learning markets and trading with an unrivalled enthusiasm. Here's to the next million, Mom!

Author's Note

These are uncertain times and that is why I congratulate you on picking up this book. Anyone actively trading markets today has some tough questions to grapple with on a regular basis.

Why do markets react so positively to bad news now? Are we at the end of a cyclical bull market or at the start of a secular bull? If the market crashes, will I lose my shirt? And if I'm not in the market, will I miss out on another banner year of gains? Are there early warning signals that will help me figure all this out?

I'm pleased to say that in fact there are. And that is why I decided to write this book.

I think I speak not only for myself when I say that good, reliable sources of information are hard to come by. We live in an age of abundant, undocumented, and sometimes ill-advised advice that flows freely across the internet.

Even the financial news can't always be trusted. It's as driven by shock and awe as any of the most questionable reality TV shows. The unvarnished fact remains that for every pundit spouting one perspective, there are just as many willing to take an opposite position. You just can't rely on what you hear.

It was out of this frustration, and out of my desire to distill truth from noise, that I embarked on this journey. I figured I wasn't the only trader whose head was reeling from the contradictory and at times downright misleading sound bites masquerading as fact out there.

So I went out in search of the latest and greatest research and best thinking on what really impacts markets. This book compiles that knowledge into a handy guidebook. If you use it wisely, it can help you gain an edge that could be the difference between winning and losing money in the markets.

Most important though, it will help you tease apart fact from fiction as you follow current trends in search of actionable news.

How would you like to know:

- The only economic indicators you need to watch each month to understand if we're headed for a correction or worse
- The way the relationship between bond prices and equities has been turned on its head
- What one commodity you should track to get an early view of the health of the economy
- How to make sense of statistical indicators like VIX and SKEW
- The two main ways markets react to geopolitical news and how you can reduce your risk even in the scariest of times
- The underutilized tool to get insight into smart money and their actions so you can trade like the pros
- The one simple rule for understanding short term momentum in markets
- How to interpret Advance/Decline lines so you don't get whipsawed
- Why risk management is the real holy grail of trading
- And so much more...

So, if that sounds good to you, I invite you to pull up a chair and join me for this exploration into the critical macroeconomic factors every good trader lives and profits by.

Enjoy the book!
Kara Boniecka

"Weak minds sink under prosperity as well as adversity; but strong and deep ones have two highest tides – when the moon is at the full, and when there is no moon." –Augustus Hare, British author

Background: A Sign of the Times

We're at a unique time in history right now. Amid the housing and financial crisis of 2008, the world went topsy-turvy. Bank bailouts and extraordinary Fed actions became commonplace. I think most people would agree that the easy money policies of the Fed have driven the prices of many asset classes up with little consideration to inherent value. We're all still waiting to see how the reining in of the good times and the reversal of quantitative easing will ultimately impact markets.

While it is impossible to have a crystal ball into the future that will predict how all these factors will unfold, one thing remains certain. The guy with the best strategy will win. And now's the time to ask... have you given ample thought to what your strategy will be should we face a market correction or worse?

After the cataclysm of 2008 and the subsequent decline in equity values, we are many years into a nice bull run. The climb has been orderly with minimal volatility and downside. But now most are beginning to wonder just how long this uptrend can last. Many are even calling for a modest correction to give this market more room to grow. The question remains, will we get a reasonable correction of 10-15% or are we in for a crash?

When the market begins to show signs of exhaustion and you no longer feel 100% confident in the direction of the trend it's a good time to have a game plan.

It's perfectly all right in the short term to keep hoping that all will be well and the market will march on to higher heights. As they say, hope springs eternal.

But remember, the higher the market goes, the more dangerous it can become. Because with an unabated rise, when the fall finally comes, it can be rough riding for all but those who are prepared.

So how prepared are you? Do you have your game plan? Are you willing to take the action needed to protect your capital? Do you know the steps you need to take to get prepared? It's not hard to do, but it does take some commitment on your part.

The simple steps outlined here and in future chapters will put you well on the road to being prepared for any future market pullbacks.

NEXT STEPS: DEVELOPING YOUR BEAR MARKET ACTION PLAN

1. Learn the warning signals you should be monitoring on a regular basis.
2. Rigorously research and determine what your bear market game plan will be BEFORE the market takes a dive and panic sets in.
3. Identify what triggers you need to see in the market to give you the green light to activate your plan.
4. Commit to sticking to your plan even through the chatter of the pundits and news media.

I went through this very process myself earlier in the year when the market started looking soft. And it was as a result of going through this process that I compiled much of the research in this book.

I put in dozens of hours creating a comprehensive checklist of warning signals and determining my personal bear market game plan. The good news for you is that I'm going to share my step-by-step process so you don't have to go through the same painstaking exercise.

And just in case you don't believe that now is the time to get into action, have a look at some of the latest warning signs:

- Experts predict that over the next decade or less, average equity gains could be brought as low as 3% per year.
- Growth in new and overseas markets that was supposed to boost equity values has been flagging.
- Hedges against market losses are being bought at a faster pace than in 2008.

- Sentiment indicators are showing increasing signs of pessimism amongst smart money while at the same time showing dangerous levels of exuberance among pundits.
- Fundamental macroeconomic factors have come in weaker than expected and yet, the market marches higher with worryingly thin volumes.

Is a bear market around the corner? It's too early to say. It's not unheard of for the market to go this long without a pullback of at least 10%. There have been four other bull runs through history which were even longer than what we're currently experiencing. The longest of the four took seven years before it faced a correction. But that was the exception and not the rule.

Months without a 10% Pullback (Closing Basis)			
Start	Top	Total Months	Years
October-90	October-97	84	7.0
March-03	October-07	54	4.5
June-62	February-66	44	3.7
June-84	August-87	38	3.2
November-11	September-14*	34	2.8
July-50	January-53	30	2.5
September-53	September-55	24	2.0
December-87	October-89	22	1.8
October-57	August-59	21	1.8
August-82	October-83	14	1.2

*Current

When the correction finally does come we could see losses of 20%, 30%, even 50% of value. During those pullback periods, there are many traders who end up blindsided and sustaining heavy losses. Given the nature of our current run-up, there is every reason to be concerned as the Fed begins to unwind its balance sheet and easy money disappears.

Start	Top	Total Months	Years	Correction
October-90	October-97	84	7.0	-11%
March-03	October-07	54	4.5	-56%
June-62	February-66	44	3.7	-16%
June-84	August-87	38	3.2	-33%
November-11	???	34	2.8	TBD
July-50	January-53	30	2.5	-10%
September-53	September-55	24	2.0	-11%
December-87	October-89	22	1.8	-10%
October-57	August-59	21	1.8	-14%
August-82	October-83	14	1.2	-14%
			Average	-20%
			Median	-14%

Keep in mind that it's not always easy to determine when a bear market has actually begun. They come in two primary ways – with a whimper or with a bang. With the latter, there is typically a major break in the market that can be hard to explain. The media will rush to Monday-night quarterback and pin the move on any number of factors, some more accurate than others.

The market break is followed by a crash, a spiraling down of prices for investors as pessimism and fear takes hold. By the time you get to this point, the pundits and financial media are loathe to accept any responsibility. The experts who cheered on small investors to buy, buy, buy, now hide behind such statements as "no one saw it coming!"

This is a painful scenario to be sure. But there are usually clear warning signals before the crash happens. Those who are paying close attention can put their bear market game plan in place early and preserve precious capital.

In the second scenario, when the bear starts with a whimper, it's much trickier to detect. The market starts to meander. There's usually increased volatility with more short lived and painful pullbacks. Increasingly, you'll see the red flag of new highs on lower volumes. The number of stocks making new highs gets smaller and smaller.

Eventually there will be the straw that breaks the camel's back and then the market will snap. We may not know what the catalyst will be, but there will be one.

Even with the many red flags we've already seen, many choose to see only that which they want to believe. History does repeat itself and it pays to learn. Better to identify the clues of a coming bear trend early than to put off taking action and merely hope for continued good times.

"By failing to prepare, you are preparing to fail." —*Benjamin Franklin, Founding Father*

Chapter 1

Are You Ready?

While the threat of a correction or worse may seem heightened at this moment in time, panicking and fear is never the solution. Even for the optimists among us it is important to plan for the worst case scenario.

The good news is that there is still time to get your plan of action in place. For exactly how long we may not know. However, each day brings an opportunity to learn new ideas that combined will contribute to your wealth of knowledge.

In this book, you will learn to prepare not only for the coming correction or bear market, but also to develop the requisite skills and an eye for market clues that will help you improve your trading generally and grow your profits overall. This information will help you make the most out of any pullback the market experiences.

As we try to make sense of the current market environment, one of the best places to start is with the economy. You may already know that the stock market broadly follows the economy, especially after accounting for short-term volatility. But you may not realize a very key distinction – the market follows *where it believes the economy is headed*, not where it has been. This more than anything else should inform the way you interpret **macro conditions** and **key indicators**.

MARKET PRINCIPLE:
The market follows where it believes the economy is headed, not where it has been. Keep this perspective firmly in view.

Once we have a good view on these economic factors, we need to understand how to **manage the risks** that are inherent in any market and how to **prepare psychologically** for the situations that may ensue. One by one, we'll look at the Macro Conditions, Key Indicators, Risk Management, and Psychology Factors that will hone your trading and give you an edge today and in the future.

"It is no crime to be ignorant of economics, which is, after all, a specialized discipline and one that most people consider to be a 'dismal science.' But it is totally irresponsible to have a loud and vociferous opinion on economic subjects while remaining in this state of ignorance." –Murray N. Rothbard, American Economist of the Austrian School

Chapter 2
All Eyes on the Economy

A careful look at the economy is the first step on the road to finding solutions for the volatility and uncertainty of a correction or bear market. To understand the economy, there are a number of macroeconomic indicators that you should follow.

Every month, dozens of numbers and statistics are released that purport to tell a story of the health of the economy. While the release may make for good news and the subsequent chatter by talking heads for good stories throughout the day, not all of these statistics will actually help you determine how to plan your trading and investing in the short and medium term.

Some of these economic reports actually tell you very little about where the economy is headed. In fact, a whole class of macro factors, so called trailing indicators, is designed to review past performance. While these may be useful for economists to do their research, the majority actually can create confusion and churn in the markets.

There are a handful of trailing indicators that are of value when trying to understand market movement. The reason they have an impact is because traders and investors realize two things: i. that the Fed determines its monetary policy, in part, based on the recent performance of the economy, and, ii. that the current and future direction of monetary policy impacts the movements of markets (I'll explain more on this in Chapter 2).

Generally speaking, for an economic indicator to have predictive value it must be current, have a clear relationship to future economic performance and lastly, discount current values with respect to future expectations.

MARKET PRINCIPLE:
For any economic indicator to have predictive value, it must be current, have a clear relationship to future economic performance, and lastly, discount current values with respect to future expectations. This is true of both leading and trailing indicators.

Leading indicators work as early warning signals of economic activity. They tend to be input oriented (production of goods that will create value downstream) and harder to measure. However, these data are deemed to be pulling the economy and therefore give an indication of where the economy is headed.

Copious research has been done to try to determine which numbers have real predictive value for future stock market values. You wouldn't necessarily know which numbers merit careful consideration from the coverage in the financial media because they must report on every number. However, there are many macroeconomic factors that may have limited relevance for you as a trader.

As with so many things in life, the 80/20 rule applies. In this time of information overload, it's helpful to focus on the most meaningful factors so you can be nimble in your response to changing market currents.

The table below shows a list of the top leading and trailing macroeconomic indicators along with the factors researchers from top universities found to have actual predictive value.

Macro-economic indicators

Trailing	Leading
■ Change in GDP	■ Stock market
■ Income & Wages	■ Manufacturing activity
✓ **Unemployment rate / jobless claims**	■ Inventory levels
✓ **CPI (inflation)**	■ Retail sales
■ Currency strength	■ Building permits
■ Interest rates	✓ **Housing market**
■ Corporate profits	■ Level of new business startups
✓ **Balance of Trade**	✓ **M1 / M2 (money supply)**
■ Value of gold/silver relative to the US dollar	✓ **PPI**
	✓ **ISM's PMI**
	✓ **Consumer credit**

Bolded factors have been found to have statistically significant predictive value.

Tracking eight indicators over the course of a month is still a fair amount, but it is much more manageable than trying to follow the dozens that are actively reported.

Let's have a more in-depth look at the indicators that are directly affecting the direction in which the economy is bound to take.

1. Unemployment Rate and the Level of Full Employment

Although the monthly jobs number is a trailing indicator, it is also one of the most impactful when it comes to market movement. This is because the Fed is watching unemployment rates very closely to determine if the economy is operating at peak performance.

MARKET PRINCIPLE:
The monthly jobs number is a trailing indicator but it is critical to watch because the Fed uses it to determine if the economy is operating at peak performance or if it must take corrective monetary action to help improve conditions.

The Fed, through its monetary policy actions, is aiming to hit what is called NAIRU, the non-accelerating inflation rate of unemployment. Currently many Fed officials put this figure in the 5.2% to 5.5% range.

When unemployment is higher than this, it implies slack in the economy. In this situation, the Fed will take action to provide stimulus in the form of lowering interest rates. More recently, the Fed has had to take other extraordinary measures like quantitative easing to help stabilize the economy. These so called accommodative actions increase the flow of money in the economy and to many asset classes such as equities.

As unemployment rates fall to the level of full employment, the cost of wages is increased. Labor costs account for approximately 70% of production expenses in America. Therefore, any increase in wages generally translates into increases in production costs. These increased costs are then passed onto the consumer in the form of higher prices for goods and services.

Typically, economists have some prediction for where the labor market is headed and most large institutions have already baked in these expectations. Any unexpected movement in the unemployment rates can spark immediate financial turmoil as traders rush to price in new expectations of future economic growth.

2. Consumer Price Index

This indicator broadly shows the rate of inflation in the US. While some inflation is a good thing, it can be extremely detrimental to economic growth if it spirals out of control. The Fed is aiming for a Goldilocks level of price increase – not too high and not too low.

Markets care about CPI because they already know that the Fed will take action if prices are not growing at an optimal level. If inflation grows too fast, the markets are bound to factor in economic policy that will slow growth. If there is recession and prices are contracting, there will be an anticipation of a recovery before it even occurs. In this case, equity prices will rise even before the recession ends. This creates an interesting conundrum – that at times it can appear that the stock market is leading the economy because of its preemptive reaction to expected Fed policy.

MARKET PRINCIPLE:
CPI is another trailing indicator that has predictive value. Traders watch CPI because they already know that the Fed will take action if prices and by proxy, inflation, is not growing at an optimal level.

---

3. Balance of Trade

Balance of trade is defined as the net difference between the exports and imports of a country. When there are more exports and more money comes into the economy, the country is said to have a trade surplus. But when there is more importing and more money going out of the country, then there is a trade deficit.

While a trade surplus can be good, when it increases too much, it may signal that the country may not be taking the best opportunities to purchase from other countries. In a global economy, nations specialize in manufacturing those products with which they have competitive and cost advantages and then buy the goods other nations produce at a cheaper, more efficient rate. In theory, this should make everyone better off as goods flow from centers of competency across the globe.

When there is a trade deficit then there can be reason to worry. Deficits can lead to significant debt. And too much debt can devalue the local currency and lessen demand for it over time. Additionally, more debt means a greater burden for future generations to shoulder. This is troublesome because it can impede the level of future economic growth.

MARKET PRINCIPLE:
Persistent trade deficits can be worrisome because they can lead to substantial national debt. This in turn can lead to a greater financial burden for future generations and can impede the levels of future economic growth.

The Balance of Trade is a more slowly moving indicator but still one worth heeding to understand the flow of money in and out of the economy in the medium and near term. As a trader, you have to interpret the most current trends in trade surpluses/deficits in terms of impact to the economy at large.

4. Housing Markets

Housing prices can move markets because of their integral connection to the consumer. For many individuals, real estate is a store of value. It can impact people's feelings of wealth and well-being and alter their comfort with spending on other goods in the economy.

Additionally, housing and real estate in general is a generator of income through associated markets like construction, realty, and mortgage lending. When housing demand is on the rise, this positively impacts prices and trickles through the overall economy.

MARKET PRINCIPLE:
Housing and real estate have an impact on equity markets for two primary reasons: i. many workers are dependent on this sector for income, and ii. consumers' perception of personal wealth, and therefore willingness to spend on other goods, is often tied to their home values.

Declines in housing prices can have a dampening effect on the economy. There are several things that could contribute to declines in housing prices. There could be more supply than demand or recent prices may have grown too high too fast, vastly outpacing inflation. The extreme case of this is when real estate markets experience a bubble. In any of these cases, there is often a need for a correction which can then lead to contraction in GDP.

The collapse of the real estate market in 2007 is widely blamed for the subsequent recession and sell-off in markets. Whatever the case may be, decline in housing prices has negative effects on the economy through these factors:

- Decreased homeowner wealth
- More unemployment due to fewer construction jobs
- Less resources for the government due to lower collections of property tax
- Declining net worth of banks and consumers as some homeowners, wanting to sell their homes, are unable and instead opt for foreclosure

Combined changes in housing values can provide a key window into where the economy is headed and by proxy the future direction of markets.

5. Money Supply

This is the disposable money available in any given economy. Different subsets of money are aggregated into various designations, generally based on the liquidity of their supply.

- M0: the dollar value of any physical cash or coin. This is the most liquid
- M1: includes all of M0 and in addition, checking accounts, traveler's checks as well as demand deposits

- M2: includes all of M1, and savings accounts, money deposits such as certificates of deposit that account for less than $100,000 and lastly, money market funds which are held by investors

The M2 is the aggregate that most traders watch as it is the most inclusive, stable, and the best representation of actual liquid currency available for trade. While in the past, an increase in the amount of money supplied to the economy meant growth in spending patterns, it could also signal inflation to come. When money supply rapidly outpaces economic growth then there are many more dollars being used to purchase the same amount of goods as before.

MARKET PRINCIPLE:
When money supply rapidly outpaces economic growth then there are many more dollars being used to purchase the same amount of goods as before. This can be the precursor to inflation run amok.

As Nobel-Prize laureate and leader of the Chicago school of economics, Milton Friedman famously said, "Inflation is always and everywhere a monetary phenomenon in the sense that it is and can be produced only by a more rapid increase in the quantity of money than in output. A steady rate of monetary growth at a moderate level can provide a framework under which a country can have little inflation and much growth. It will not produce perfect stability; it will not produce heaven on earth; but it can make an important contribution to a stable economic society."

6. Producer Price Index

The producer price index is used to show the cost of production from the seller's perspective. It shows trends within wholesale, commodity, and manufacturing markets. It is also important to note that it excludes all imports.

The monthly PPI release has three headline index figures, one each for commodity, stage-of-processing and finished goods on the national level. Traders typically focus on the core PPI figure—the finished goods index minus the food and energy components, which are removed because of their volatility. This number is of interest because increases in producers' costs may soon be passed on to the consumer and lead to higher prices in the economy.

MARKET PRINCIPLE:
Although CPI is the de facto index of inflation, PPI represents the costs producers face upstream. Therefore it provides a preview into where inflation might be headed. And as you know, any sneak peek into where the economy is headed, gives the smart trader a leg up.

The PPI is reported relative to a base year, which is 1982, and should therefore always be considered as a percentage change from the prior period. The percent change and the annual projected rate will be the most impactful figures of the release.

7. Purchasing Managers Index

The Institute for Supply Management (ISM) oversees the Purchasing Managers Index on a monthly basis by conducting a survey of more than 400 purchasing managers from diverse industries and geographies. The PMI is composed of five sub-indicators weighted as follows:

- Production level (0.25)
- New orders from customers (0.30)
- Supplier deliveries and the pace of fulfillment (0.15)
- Inventories (0.10)
- Employment level (0.20)

Although manufacturing is no longer the economic engine it once was in the US, statistics show that it is often the industry where recessions begin and end. In that regard, the PMI can give traders an early clue as to where the economy is headed.

MARKET PRINCIPLE:
Manufacturing may not be the economic engine it once was in the United States, however, statistics show that it is often the industry where recessions begin and end. In that regard, PMI can give traders an early clue as to where the economy is headed.

Research has shown that 50 is the key number to remember for the PMI; at 50 and above, the manufacturing sector is deemed to be expanding and the economy as well as GDP should be expanding as well.

Another key figure to keep in mind is 42. An index level that consistently prints higher than 42 signals positive economic sentiment. The various levels between 42 and 50 speak to the strength of the expansion. If the PMI falls below 42, there is need to be concerned as a recession might already be underway. In this way, PMI is an excellent leading indicator of where the economy and therefore the market could be headed.

8. Consumer Credit Report

This report is released on a monthly basis from the Federal Reserve. It covers the revolving and non-revolving credit used mainly for buying consumer goods. Many traders consider this indicator valuable in showing the future spending habits of consumers as well as showing the extent to which the benchmark interest rates like the fed funds rates and prime rates are manifesting themselves at the consumer levels.

This indicator is also critical because consumers account for nearly two-thirds of all GDP consumption. If there is less consumption due to unavailability of funds then GDP may not grow. And as we've covered extensively to this point, the equity markets are keenly interested in where GDP is headed.

MARKET PRINCIPLE:
Consumers account for nearly two-thirds of all GDP consumption. If their ability to consume is impeded by lack of credit this can negatively impact overall GDP and therefore the direction of markets.

The above eight macroeconomic factors are the most critical indicators to watch on a monthly basis. If you can track these numbers and observe their underlying trends, you'll have an automatic leg up on the average non-institutional trader.

The important thing is to focus on these factors and not get sucked into the spin cycle the financial media encourages at every data release. Remember, you ultimately have to make up your own mind about the economy and subsequent market direction. You now have valuable tools to help you in this endeavor. Use these wisely.

NEXT STEPS: TRACKING THE MACROECONOMIC FACTORS

1. *Create a mechanism, e.g. a spreadsheet or notebook, to track these eight key macroeconomic factors on a regular basis. (LakeshoreATS offers a twice weekly newsletter subscription that tracks these factors and others with relevant market commentary and analysis. Find more information on p. 51.)*

2. In particular, identify the long-term average, the near-term trend direction, and the most recent value.

3. Begin to observe the relationship between market movements and economic data surprises in real-time.

"Almost permanently affixed on the whiteboard of PIMCO's Investment Committee boardroom is a series of concentric circles, resembling the rings of a giant redwood...

PIMCO's Concentric Circles

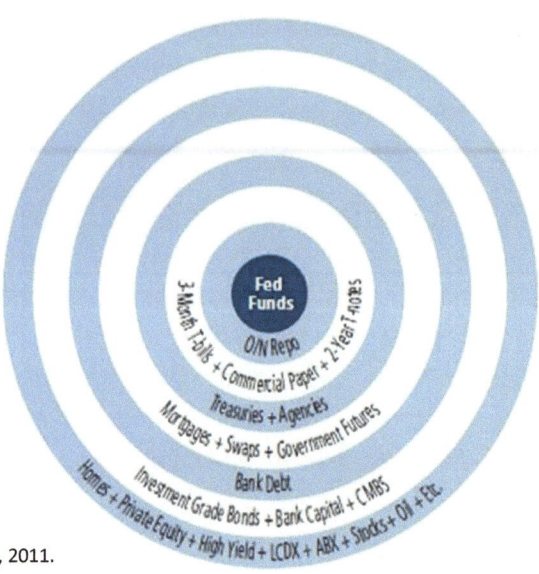

Source: PIMCO, 2011.

Our visual schematic expresses a more complicated process of cause and effect that allows an investor to anticipate price changes instead of simply describing ex post returns and volatility... ***Change the price of credit at the center and you change the price of assets at the outer extremities."*** *—Bill Gross, American financial manager and co-founder of PIMCO*

Chapter 3

Other Assets and Their Relation to Equity Prices

We've now covered the key data releases to watch on a monthly basis. Are there other factors you can watch regularly to get a preview into market direction? Absolutely.

1. Bonds

The relationship between stocks and bonds used to be fairly straightforward. Bond prices and equity prices tend to be correlated with equities generally lagging movement in bonds.

Remember that bond prices and yields always move in opposite directions. As yields decrease, bond prices increase. Also, as yields decrease, borrowing becomes less expensive and the cost of doing business is lower for companies. We would expect to see equities do well in a low-interest environment as profitability increases.

The relationship between stocks and bonds holds true in times of normal inflation and is the main reason for the run-up in both bond and equity prices immediately following the Fed's extraordinary quantitative easing (QE) measures.

Later in the credit/equity cycle, the relationship between stocks and bonds shifts. To understand this, consider the relationship between yields and dividends. The average stock pays low dividends relative to bonds and other assets, with yields around 2-3%. As interest rates rise, the low-paying and relatively risky dividends of stocks look less appealing to investors and they shift money into bonds, CDs, and the money market. The reverse is also true and what we've seen with quantitative easing – money flowing out of bonds and into equities as managers chase returns.

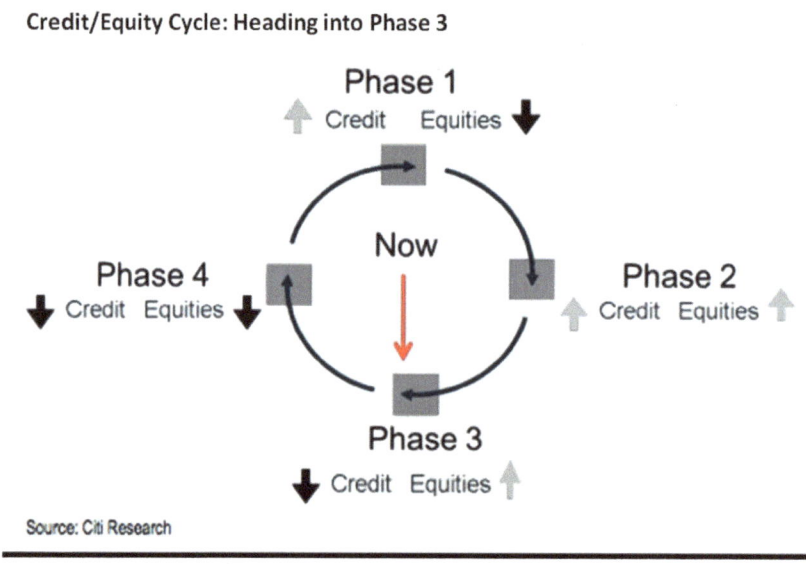

Credit/Equity Cycle: Heading into Phase 3

Source: Citi Research

For traders, the yield on the US 10-year Treasury note is the most important to watch. As with many of the macroeconomic factors, the trendline provides an important clue as to the state of the economy. When interest rates remain depressed, it means that investors are willing to pay higher prices for relatively low returns. This represents a flight to quality.

MARKET PRINCIPLE:
There are three things to keep in mind with regards to bonds. Stocks and bonds are often correlated with equities generally lagging. As yields on bonds decline, normally risk-averse investors may be forced to chase returns with riskier assets. And finally, keep an eye on the 10-Yr T-Note to gauge fearfulness among investors.

In the extreme, when bond yields fall very low, it is a sign that investors are accepting whatever meager but safe return they can get rather than demanding higher returns from other assets. When the 10-year Treasury note moves below 2.5% it is a sign that investors are increasingly worried about the state of riskier assets like equities.

2. Currency Strength and Economic Growth

Currencies and other commodities can also provide an early view into the direction the economy and markets are likely to head. These relationships are somewhat more complicated than the macroeconomic factors as there are many more things that can impact them.

Currency valuations are never decided in a vacuum. They are always considered relative to other currencies. When the US dollar is strong, then the purchasing power for US currency in foreign markets is high. Products for importation are bought cheaply and those for exportation are sold at a higher foreign price.

It might seem that it is always beneficial to have a strong currency. However, there is a small catch-22 at work; when the dollar is weak, there can be more foreign demand for products manufactured in the US and more business for US-based companies. This can be a tremendous advantage for economic growth.

Currency valuation is far from a slam-dunk indicator of equity market direction because of the noise from related factors. In general though, the value of the dollar rises in anticipation of improving business activity. However, keep in mind that only about 35-40% of the stock market's movement is correlated with that of the US dollar.

I have included currency valuation mainly so that you can discount news stories as appropriate when the financial media tries to stir the fear pot around the strengthening or weakening of the US dollar.

3. The Contribution of Precious Metals

Gold and silver are often viewed as stores of value alternate to the US dollar because many believe they have inherent value that cannot be fabricated through the machinations of monetary policy. When the economy suffers or the value of the US dollar declines, more people flock to these commodities as a safe haven. In this regard, precious metal prices can be a reflection of sentiment towards the US dollar and its future.

The relationship between precious metals and equities can be somewhat volatile as there are extraneous factors impacting peoples' desire to put money into these alternate assets. One commodity that more directly tracks the economy is copper.

Sometimes referred to as "**Dr. Copper,**" many have noted its unique ability to predict turning points in the global economy. Copper is used in nearly every sector of the economy from manufacturing and construction to technology and energy distribution.

If you are going to follow only one precious metal in relation to your equity trading, make it copper. With its multitude of uses across many sectors of the economy it can serve as a canary in the coal mine for economic slowdowns.

Its broad role across industries makes it a good leading indicator of economic health and when demand is strong, it generally means economic output will also be strong.

One thing to consider with commodity prices in general is that they are relevant on a global scale rather than to the US only. However, to the extent that the US is the largest economy in the world, they still merit some consideration.

4.   Black Gold, the Other Precious Commodity

The final commodity to consider when gauging the direction of the economy is **oil**. Many traders tend to watch the movement of the NYMEX crude oil prices closely.

The price of oil, and gasoline by proxy, can have a big impact on consumers' disposable incomes. When prices hang above $100 for too long, it increases fear of less consumer spending in other areas of the economy. Less spending means a less healthy economy and potentially bad news for equities.

This inverse relationship is not always hard and fast. In fact, about 40% of the time, oil and equities move in tandem. Part of this is because oil has a large degree of built-in seasonality and typically rises sharply in the summer only to decline in the fall. However, the main thing to remember is that when oil prices spike because of geopolitical shocks, this is typically bad for stocks.

When prices rise because other industrial commodities are also rising, this generally signals healthy economic growth, which is good for equity markets. If you keep this relationship in mind when interpreting oil prices, it will help you avoid panic simply because oil prices are rising.

"Success breeds complacency. Complacency breeds failure. Only the paranoid survive." –Andy Grove, Hungarian-American businessman and former CEO of Intel Corporation

Chapter 4

Volatility and Complacency

More and more in the financial media you hear about VIX, the so-called "investor fear gauge." To a lesser extent, but no less important, many have also begun talking about SKEW, a measure of fat tail risk in the markets.

The price of VIX is used by many traders to gauge the level of market risk. In more explicit terms, the VIX is a measure of expected volatility of 30-day returns in the S&P 500 implied by the prices of near-term options. In general, it moves inversely to the S&P 500 and typically more strongly when the market moves down.

The key values to remember for VIX are 20 and 30. When the values are below 20, then there is more orderly movement, less fear and some would even say complacency in the market. When this indicator is above 30 there is greater volatility in the market, possibly signaling a large market move in the coming weeks.

One key thing to understand about the VIX is that it is a measure of investors' willingness to hedge their equity exposure. As such, it is necessarily more potent to the downside – people are more likely to insure against bad things than good. Over the 14-year period from 1990 to 2004, a 1% increase in the S&P 500 was accompanied by a 2.3% decrease in VIX while a 1% decrease in the S&P 500 was accompanied by a 4.26% increase in VIX.

This lopsidedness in interpretation of the VIX is one reason why it is important also to look at SKEW when considering market volatility. In simple terms, SKEW measures the likelihood of negative outlier events, so called, black swans. In its history, the average value of SKEW has been 117.5. The key level to consider for SKEW is 130. Above here, be assured that smart money is taking out increased levels of insurance against a significant market sell-off.

Putting the two measures together therefore is of great value. A "low VIX/high SKEW" combination essentially says that the market overall is complacent but institutional investors believe there is far more risk of downside than usual. This is very important to note when trying to determine if the market is headed for rocky roads.

MARKET PRINCIPLE:
The combination of a low VIX and a high SKEW can be a useful indicator of rocky roads ahead in equity markets.

The opposite is also true – that high VIX/low SKEW could signal an opportunity to jump back in to markets as the fear factor has gotten unreasonably high.

Through some fairly straightforward analysis you can generate more explicit probabilities of expected 30-day market returns (e.g. A VIX/SKEW combination of 18/135 implies that market participants believe that there is a 1 in 6 chance the market will move at least 8% in next 30 and a 1 in 8 chance it will move at least 10%.) The CBOE has academic papers on both VIX and SKEW that nicely outline these steps. Also, the LakeshoreATS Equity Market Update (more information on p. 51) includes these factor calculations to show the general market willingness to pay for protection to the downside.

NEXT STEPS: TRACKING OTHER ASSET CLASSES

1. Determine which alternative asset classes or financial instruments make the most sense to track on an on-going basis in relation to the markets you trade.

2. Add these asset classes to your macroeconomic factor list.

3. Create a schedule to regularly track the movements of these assets, e.g. every Monday morning, or on the date of a key data release.

4. Create an alert (e.g. using Google alerts) that will update you of any breaking news related to these assets.

5. Maintain a healthy skepticism of reports claiming too close a relationship between the equity markets and various alternative asset classes. History and statistics simply do not bear out these hard and fast rules and more nuanced consideration of related factors is necessary.

"Too many corporations and organizations ignore political risks until it is too late. These risks are either assumed to occur rarely (or to someone else) or to be entirely unpredictable. In both cases nothing could be farther from the truth." –Bremmer & Keat in the Fat Tail: The Power of Political Knowledge for Strategic Investing

Chapter 5
Geopolitical Calculus

No book on identifying market trends before they happen would be complete without mentioning the toll geopolitical strife can take. I'm not going to talk about specific conflicts bubbling across the globe today. Instead, I want to take the long view.

Consider this, there have always been and will always be various threats, uncertainties, and ugly realities in the world. The level of geopolitical threat never goes away entirely. What changes is the amount of attention we pay to the events happening around us.

When it comes to markets, it is not the geopolitical strife that has an impact as much as new awareness of a situation and the intervening coverage that move the needle. This is by no means to say that you shouldn't pay attention to what's happening in the world.

When the world seems especially dangerous, investors tend to jump to attention, hone in on the riskiness of assets, and try to rebalance their holdings toward safer havens.

The first market casualties tend to be momentum-driven trades. This is because some percentage of people driving prices up are not fundamentally bullish but rather merely betting that there will be future buyers even more intent on getting on board. As these fair-weather investors flee for the doors, it can lead to accelerating sell-offs in the stocks they've been riding.

Next, you begin to see a broader repricing of risk as people start better to understand the nature of a threat and its implications. You can see this happen in the impacted asset classes particularly in commodities, currencies, and bonds across the globe.

Sometimes it takes a bit longer for this risk repricing to materialize in stocks, particularly if the threat is potent enough to make us worried but not imminent enough to warrant full on panic.

When risk is being repriced in equities, you see more and more people questioning valuations. Good news is ignored or discounted more heavily. Investors are less willing to pay higher multiples for stocks even when they seem justified. And you hear more statements like, "I'll wait to invest until things settle down," as the worry factor builds.

The key point to remember here is that the more extreme the threat, the closer to home, and the more imminent, the more likely markets will react hard, fast, and down.   In the case of geopolitical threats, reaction time is the most important aspect.

On seeing news of an event unfold and coverage increase, those traders first out the door typically win in the short-term. If your style of trading favors longer hold periods, it may make sense just to hold on for things to quiet down in the media.

Sample Political Analysis Matrix from Citi Research, May 2014.

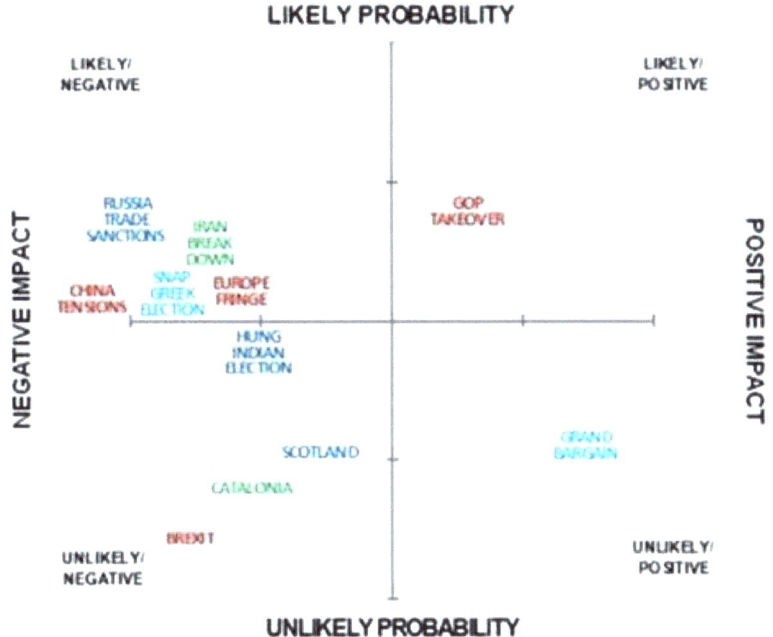

Source: Citi Research, 2014.

NEXT STEPS: ASSESSING GEOPOLITICAL RISK

1. Find a good source of geopolitical news analysis that is actively watching for conflicts brewing around the world. All the better if this source has an economic or financial perspective.

2. Consider which political news stories in the mainstream media are dominating the airwaves and internet and how the news could potentially impact the markets you are trading (e.g. The Arab Spring and the impact on oil markets trickling down to equities).

"Men, it has been well said, think in herds; it will be seen that they go mad in herds, while they only recover their senses slowly, and one by one." —Charles Mackay, 19th century Scottish poet and journalist

Chapter 6

Sentiment and Momentum

Before we move on to how to actually protect yourself during a market correction or worse, I want to spend a little time looking at the impact market participants have on the market itself through feedback loops and virtuous (vicious?) cycles of self-fulfilling prophecy.

In some ways, **sentiment** indicators can be counterintuitive. When the market is at a top, participants tend to unanimously agree on a bullish sentiment. The experts, popular analysts and the general public have all rallied around the idea that the bull market is here to stay and exuberance wins the day.

When all caution has been thrown to the wind, when you're getting stock tips from your cab driver or waitress, and when even permabears have changed their tune, it's time to head for the exits. Some may ask why such positive sentiment is exactly an indicator of bad things ahead. The answer is simple. When everyone is fully invested, there's no money left to drive prices higher.

MARKET PRINCIPLE:
Beware irrational exuberance at all costs. There is perhaps no better predictor of when markets have entered bubble territory and are speeding headlong toward a crash.

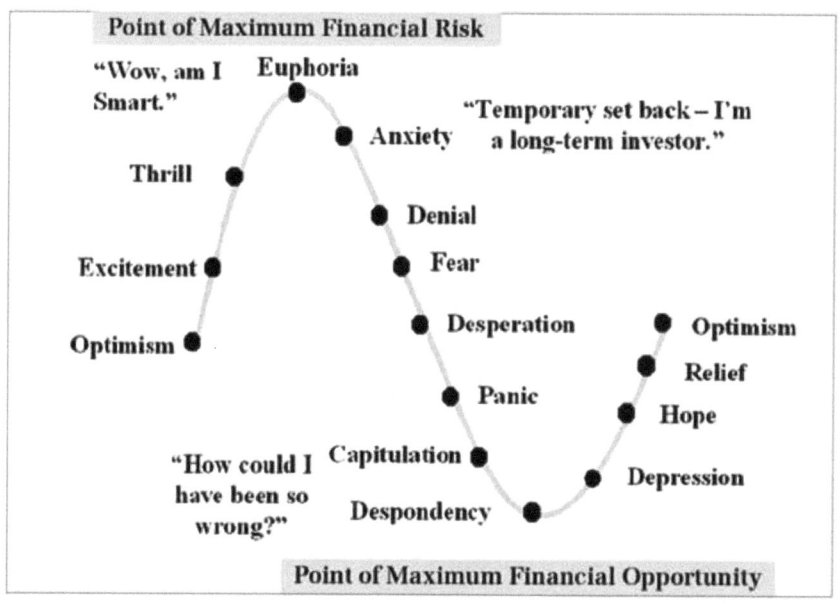

Source: The Financial Philosopher.

As an indicator, this requires a somewhat subjective call. Listen carefully for a sense that absolutely nothing can hold the market down. Phrases like, "this time is different" or "we're in a new paradigm" are generally tip-offs.

There are also other more exact measures of the level of bullish sentiment among institutional investors that you can track, such as the AAII Sentiment Survey or Investors Intelligence's Advisors' Sentiment Report.

One quick and dirty way to look for trouble in a bull market is to observe the **daily momentum**. You don't need any fancy indicators and you don't have to wait for official economic releases. Simply watch the trade in the last hour of the day. When you see repeated sell-offs before the regular floor session ends, you know the bulls have started to struggle.

An end of the day sell-off could signal that there is fear something might happen overnight, say a geopolitical phenomenon, which would work against the market. It's also a clue to the level of commitment among investors to the current level of market strength.

The opposite is also true – if the market closes on highs more often than on lows then you are bound to see more commitment from investors and continued upward movement.

Finally, sometimes you hear pundits talking about the market's **advances and declines**. This is a measure of market breadth, which tells how broad a rally is. When prices are trending strongly, the A-D line will move in the same direction as the price. If the majority of stocks are advancing as prices overall are increasing, then the rally is broad and strong. In the midst of a downturn, prices typically fall in line with the A-D line. When you observe divergences between price and market breadth, this is usually a sign of a reversal of the trend.

Many in the financial media flock to this statistic because it has good resonance with the average investor. It is easy to digest its meaning. But be careful because following breadth exclusively can lead to a number of false signals.

As an indicator, it prices in a fair amount of expectation, rather than actual predictive value. For instance, you often see the indicator move higher after a sharp price decline as traders enter the market hoping they have found a bottom. As such, it can be more valuable for understanding price action in an uptrend than a downtrend.

By no means should you rely on this to the exclusion of everything else discussed in this book, but as one more tool in your toolbox, it can help to confirm your suspicions about market movement. The rule to remember is that A/D divergences tend to be important at significant market tops.

NEXT STEPS: INCORPORATING MARKET SENTIMENT

1. Identify 2-3 sentiment indicators you will follow on a regular basis and add to your factor list. *(LakeshoreATS offers a twice weekly newsletter subscription that tracks these factors and others with relevant market commentary and analysis. Find more information on p. 51.)*

2. Observe the market movement in the last hour of trade for a quick and dirty gauge of strength of the trend.

"Risk is a function of how poorly a strategy will perform if the 'wrong' scenario occurs." –Michael Porter, Professor of Strategy and Competitiveness at Harvard Business School

Chapter 7

Risk Management

Risk management is an essential part of every successful trading program. Particularly when trading through a correction or bear market, you must pay keen attention to managing your risks. As always, the number one rule is to **identify potential risks** and **practice good position sizing**. But keep in mind that good risk management should be an on-going process rather than a one-off exercise.

The Cycle of Risk Management

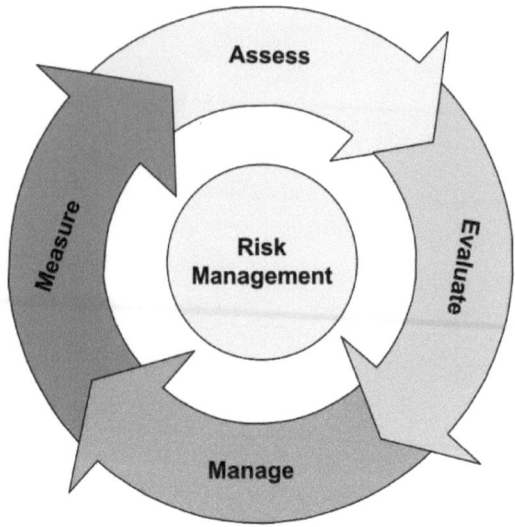

You should always have your maximum downside identified and strictly adhere to your pre-determined trading plan. Once you have done this, turn your attention to position sizing. Simply put, as you have more wins, scale your positions up and as you have losses, scale back in an orderly and also pre-determined fashion. This will help you preserve your capital through good times and bad and make sure you have enough in reserve to get back into markets when things turn around.

MARKET PRINCIPLE:
Good risk management is a beautiful thing. Great risk management is the real holy grail of trading – it can take a mediocre system and make it profitable. Ignore it at your peril.

When a downturn is looming, you should **get or stay defensive**. Whatever this means for your chosen style of trading – be it through hedging, reallocation of holdings, or even being prepared to move into cash. Figure out your plan to act through a downturn and commit to sticking with it.

Next, it is extremely important to **protect your principal**. Do not be afraid of incurring trading costs and capital gains taxes if it means preserving capital. For more active traders, better to take a small loss if the market is turning than to double down on losers hoping for better days.

Diversification is crucial to managing risk. The idea here is to spread your allocations around so that you are not overexposed to any particular asset. The important thing to note is that these different assets must be negatively correlated. In other words, when one falls, the other rises.

For active traders, perhaps this means keeping some of your total net worth in assets that are not correlated with the markets you trade. It may take a little work on your part to investigate which areas these constitute, but it is well worth it for the peace of mind it offers during times of market turmoil.

My final piece of advice is to **be patient.** In the history of equity markets, one thing has proven always to be true. Things will eventually turn around. And those that manage to keep their wits about them in times of confusion generally profit the most.

NEXT STEPS: REASSESSING YOUR RISK CONTROLS

1. For every system or strategy that you trade, identify your risk plan. Memorialize it on paper and put it someplace where you can always see it while trading.

2. Commit to sticking to your trading plan, getting out of losing trades as proscribed, rather than holding on to see if the market will turn.

3. If appropriate, consider adding defensive positions to your portfolio to help you weather a downturn.

"Anyone who claims to be intrigued by the 'intellectual challenge of the markets' is not a trader. The markets are as intellectually challenging as a fistfight...Ultimately, trading is an exercise in self-mastery and endurance." –Ralph Vince, Money Manager and Quant

Chapter 8
Putting on Your Game Face

Having a winning psychology is without doubt one of the most important aspects of trading. Among both novice and experienced traders, many a mistake has been made on the basis of emotions. Long before the market turns, you should understand that in times of a correction or bear market, emotions will be heightened. You need to be prepared with mechanisms to react to and control your emotions.

Although you may already be familiar with the four psychological states most relevant for trading, it pays to review. Greed, fear, hope and regret combined are responsible for the largest percentage of trading errors and missteps than any single macroeconomic factor we discussed above.

MARKET PRINCIPLE:
Think long and hard about the psychological baggage you bring to your trading before the market forces your hand.

When your emotional landscape is compromised, you are no longer in control and able to make good assessments of risk and reward. However, when your emotions are your allies, then you're in the driver's seat and in a better position to profit even through the roughest of market conditions.

The dictionary defines **greed** as "the excessive desire for money and/or wealth." When taken in the context of trading, it means that one has a desire to make abnormally large profits in a relatively short amount of time.

Traders who are driven by greed focus on how much money they have already made, and how much more they could make if they stay in a particular position. What they sometimes forget in the excitement of the chase is that profits are made only on the closure of a trade. Until then, paper profits remain strictly potential profits.

The downfall of the greedy is improper risk management. When things look good, caution is thrown to the wind. Sometimes it works out in their favor, but in the long run, that old market saying is true, "Bulls make money, bears make money but pigs get slaughtered."

Fear is a very powerful emotion that can cripple anyone and lead to poor decision making. When fear sets in, panic is not far behind. And once panic has taken hold it is nearly impossible to make decisions soberly.

Every trader needs to realize that fear is an emotional reaction to a perceived threat. A critical analysis of what causes fear in the moment might reveal that there is minimal threat after all!

Always be prepared to analyze what you're afraid of and why. These questions will help you stay calm and work through any market environment to your favor.

Hope may be the most dangerous emotion of all when it comes to trading. When you hang onto a trade far beyond your pre-determined maximum loss, hoping that the tides will turn, it's time to take a break.

A trading plan is put in place to help you contain your downside risk and preserve your capital. You can hardly live to trade another day if you blow your capital on an emotion-hazed whim. Be realistic, adhere to your plan, and keep hope in check.

After greed has seen you hold a position too long, and fear has set in as it turns against you, and finally hope that it will turn around again has dissolved into thin air – only then comes **regret**. This is a feeling of disappointment and sadness over an occurrence that did not go as planned or desired.

Understand that there will be times when a trade doesn't work out, or when the market moves against you. The danger for traders comes when they get caught up in focusing on the losses or missed opportunities for winning trades.

For the overall well-being of your mind and your capital, the best thing you can do is to evaluate the situation, learn from your mistakes and then move on. Trade for the long haul and in the end you will win.

Never underestimate the power that psychology can have on your trading. In the best of bull markets, you may feel cocky and invincible, but there's nothing like a correction to reveal your weaknesses. Get your frame of mind in order long before you need to react and it will pay untold dividends.

There are many ways to take psychology out of the equation – meditation, automation, simulation, to name a few. Make use of any or all of these techniques to protect your interests and your capital.

NEXT STEPS: PUTTING YOUR PSYCHOLOGICAL HOUSE IN ORDER

1. Spend some time considering those times when trades have not gone your way. If possible, really try to relive the feelings you experienced. What action did you take? If you had to do it over again, what would you do differently? Be brutally honest with yourself. The market certainly will be.

2. If you don't already keep a trade log, consider documenting your wins and losses as well as the emotions that you feel as the positions unfold.

3. Read a book about the ways in which psychology can negatively impact trading profitability (e.g. Mark Douglas' The Disciplined Trader) and determine which strategies might work best for you.

"Acknowledge the complexity of the world and resist the impression that you easily understand it. People are too quick to accept conventional wisdom, because it sounds basically true and it tends to be reinforced by both their peers and opinion leaders, many of whom have never looked at whether the facts support the received wisdom. It's a basic fact of life that many things 'everybody knows' turn out to be wrong." -Jim Rogers

Chapter 9

Final Thoughts

While there are signs pointing to a worrying trend, we may not yet be in a place to act. It is important that you follow the guidelines shared in this book to determine how to prepare for the future.

In a summary;

- ➤ Lay out your market correction / bear market game plan
- ➤ Track the key early warning signals we've laid out above
- ➤ Manage your emotions and stick to your strategy
- ➤ Be prudent when making any changes in real time
- ➤ Keep your attention firmly planted on risk management

These simple rules will keep you in good stead through bull markets and bear, through good times and bad.

When markets turn, hang in there. Remember that in the end, it pays not to panic.

Finally, I end this book with a bit of history. Consider this. The modern US stock market has experienced just five major bear markets in a nearly hundred year period (1929-1932; 1937-1941; 1973-1974; 2000-2002; and 2008).

Looking at the magnitude of declines, statistics show that while losses have been as great as 64% in the most severe of pullbacks, the average loss was in the 35-40% range.

Next, keep in mind that snapbacks are often as violent and sometimes as unexpected as crashes. Average equity returns following a bear market were up to 3x higher than their long-term averages. When you sit on the sidelines in fear of market moves, you run the risk of missing out on these highly profitably times.

So, get your game plan in order and watch attentively for the signals. And remember that while we prepare for the future, it is in the here and now that we must live and act.

To your well-being and wealth...
Happy trading, traders!

Kara Boniecka

SPECIAL BONUS OFFER

Two Month Subscription to
the LakeshoreATS Market Digest
for Free!

As a thank you for purchasing *Identifying Market Tops: the Macro Factors Every Smart Trader Lives By*, LakeshoreATS would like to offer you a two month subscription to its twice weekly market newsletter. That's a total value of $49.98 – for free!

Within the digest, we actively follow the macro factors outlined above and provide relevant and concise commentary on the news stories and numbers that are moving markets today.

Now you don't have to update and track these factors on your own. Stay in the know with our convenient newsletter so you never have to worry about missing key data and news.

To begin your subscription, simply register today at
http://www.lakeshoreats.com/newsletter-signup.

Within the LakeshoreATS Market Digest, you'll learn many things, not least of which:

- Latest macroeconomic data releases that you must follow to understand where markets are headed
- A review of historical ranges, recent trends, and most current value of these factors

- Relevant commentary on under-the-radar news that could impact your trading in days or weeks to come
- An overview of key trading levels for the S&P 500 futures market
- An interpretation of the latest VIX/SKEW numbers in plain English
- The latest sentiment statistics from smart money
- A perspective into market breadth and momentum
- And so much more...

Whether you are a sophisticated trader with years under your belt or a novice just entering the market, there is a wealth of knowledge in this digest. We take the effort and challenge out of tracking these macro factors on an on-going basis. This absolutely will change your view of markets. Register now at http://www.lakeshoreats.com/newsletter-signup.

INDEX

Acknowledgements

Over the years my mother has encouraged me to put pen to paper. I'm not sure this is the book she was expecting to see, alas, life is unpredictable that way.

First, I thank my husband, Tom, for his unwavering support and belief in me. At the times when I've been most vulnerable to succumbing to the psychological strain of trading – greed, fear, and regret were constant companions in the early days – he has encouraged me to carry on. Through this perseverance I have had the privilege to refine my skills and develop trading systems in which I truly believe.

Next, I would like to thank my wonderful family. My parents, who worked so hard to give me every advantage in life but also taught me to be humble and grateful for each opportunity afforded me. My older sister, who through her example taught me that a modern woman could have it all – loving family, pursuit of purpose, and a dynamic social life. And my younger brother, who is wise beyond his years and generous beyond belief.

I thank my dear friend Erlinda Vo Lieberman, who has been with me on this fun-filled journey toward each fulfilling her life's dream. To my team of researchers and designers I owe a debt for whipping this book into shape. And to Melissa Wilson, for so graciously offering her thoughts on how best to get this book into your hands.

As Helen Keller said, "Alone we can do so little, together we can do so much."

About the Author

Kara Boniecka's love of finance and markets goes back to her earliest days. She fondly remembers playing "banker" with her stuffed animals and being thrilled at age 7 to be given responsibility to go inside Bell Federal Bank to submit her parents' mortgage payment.

As she grew older, she honed her financial acumen through academic rigor. She graduated from Harvard University at age 19 with an AB in applied math with economics. Later, she attended the Wharton School at the University of Pennsylvania where she obtained an MBA in finance and graduated top 5% in her class.

Boniecka has worked for many top financial firms in both financial modeling and systems design capacities. She started her trading career in the grain pits at the CBOT, before moving on to work at a bulge bracket bank and finally at a proprietary trading shop in Chicago.

Her background has afforded her a keen focus on risk management and capital appreciation. Since 2010, she has been developing and trading her own automated systems. Her expertise in algorithm development and advanced data sciences techniques has made her the perfect fit for quant/mechanical trading. However, she believes wholeheartedly in a balanced approach that utilizes macro analysis to increase trade performance.

It was out of the desire to help others make sense of markets that she wrote this book.

Copyright